Follow The FOOD CHAIN

Who ate the Butterfly?

A RAINFOREST FOOD CHAIN

Sarah Ridley

WAYLAND
www.waylandbooks.co.uk

First published in Great Britain in 2019
by Wayland

Designer: Lisa Peacock
Editor: Nicola Edwards

HB ISBN: 978 1 5263 1230 3
PB ISBN: 978 1 5263 1231 0

Printed and bound in China

Wayland, an imprint of
Hachette Children's Group
Part of Hodder and Stoughton
Carmelite House
50 Victoria Embankment
London EC4Y 0DZ
An Hachette UK Company
www.hachette.co.uk
www.hachettechildrens.co.uk

MIX
Paper from
responsible sources
FSC® C104740
www.fsc.org

Picture acknowledgements
iStock: OG Stock 17t; Raciro 6bc, 7t,
8bc,12bc,14bc, 16bcl,18bcl, 20bc; Marek
Stefunko 11b, 22bc.
Nature PL: Sebastian Kennerknecht 15t; Chien
Lee 19t; Bence Mate 13; Chris Mattison 5b.
Shutterstock: Gerry Bishop 22cl; Julio Alberto
Bragado 6c; Lukas Budinsky 9c; Juhku1;
Gmlykin 4; Bob Hilscher 23cr; Matt Jeppson
23b; Laranik 12t, 12br, 14br,16br, 18br,
21cl, 22tr; Inga Locmele 5t; Jon Nicholls
Photography 10b; Peter Niesen 18t, 19bcr,
21cr, 23tc; Nnattali 22b; Omariam front cover
bl; PhotocechCZ 16t, 17bc, 19bcl, 21br, 23cl;
Ondrej Prosicky 11t,14,15bl, 17bl, 19bl, 21bl,
22br; Sumruay Rattanataipob 2; Alex Reiff
front cover br; Tanguy de Saint-Cyr10t, 23tl;
Schaef712bcrt, 8t, 8bclt, 14bcrt, 16bct,
18bcrt, 20brt, 22crt; Nattawit Sronrachrudee
6bl,
8bl, 12bl, 14bl,16bl, 18bl, 20cl; Universal
Wallpapers front cover tr, 8bcrb, 9t, 12bcrb,
14bcrb, 16bcb,18bcrb, 20brb, 22crb; Tony
Wear front cover tl; Wildnerdpix 7c.

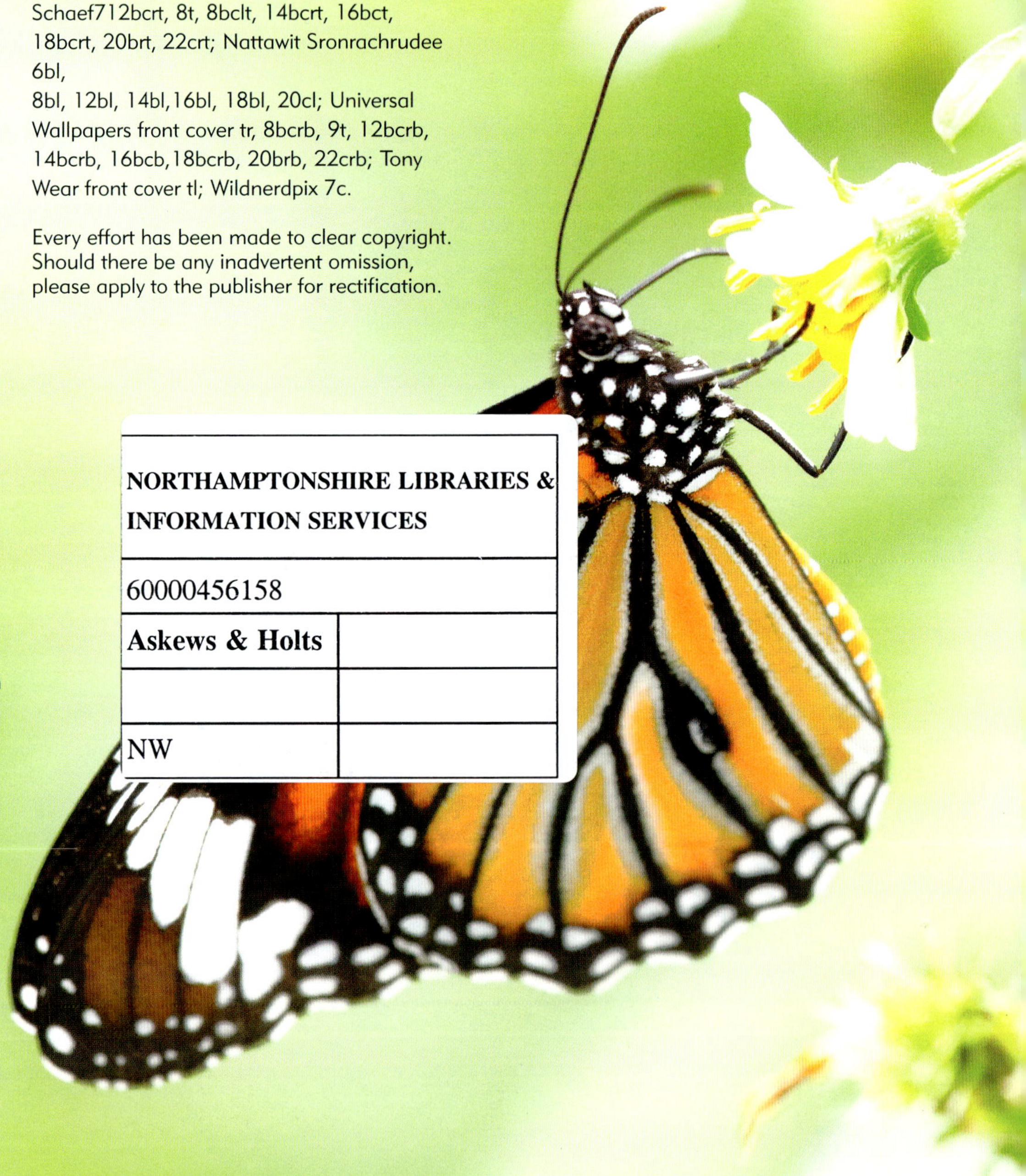

CONTENTS

Food for life   4

The start of the food chain   6

Who ate the leaf?   8

What else eats rainforest plants?   10

Who ate the butterfly?   12

Who ate the lizard?   14

Who ate the opossum?   16

Who ate the ocelot?   18

Follow a rainforest food chain   20

A rainforest food web   22

Useful words   24

Index   24

Food for life

All living things need food to give them the **energy** to live, or they will die. Plants make their own food using energy from sunlight, air and water. They are called **producers** because they produce – or make – their own food.

Rainforests are full of plants. They fill the space with their green leaves.

Animals cannot make their own food so they have to eat plants, or other animals that eat plants. They are called **consumers** because they consume – or eat – plants and animals.

Butterflies, ants, beetles and hummingbirds like to eat the **nectar** of passion flowers.

Producers and consumers are linked together by many different food chains. It all depends on what eats what. This book looks at a **food chain** in a Central American **rainforest**.

This red-eyed tree frog is eating a spider.

The start of the food chain

At the start, or bottom, of every food chain are plants. Thousands of different plants live in rainforests. They grow well in places that are warm, sunny and wet.

▼In a food chain, an arrow shows the food energy moving from one living thing to another.

The leaves of plants are where they make their food using sunlight, water and air. The tallest trees get lots of sunlight but less reaches plants growing on the forest floor.

How many different sorts of leaf can you see?

Lots of plants grow on other plants in rainforests.

The roots of a **bromeliad** hold onto a tree.

?   ?   ?

Who ate the leaf?

A caterpillar ate the leaf.

The caterpillar eats lots of leaves until it is time to change into …

The blue morpho caterpillar likes to eat the leaves of peas and other plants.

… a blue morpho butterfly. Now it drinks food by sucking up liquid from trees and rotting **fruit** and animals!

The butterfly's bright blue wings help it find a mate. When it closes its wings (right), the brown colour hides it from predators.

What else eats rainforest plants?

High in the treetops, howler monkeys walk from branch to branch eating flowers, fruit and leaves.

Lots of rainforest animals eat plants.

A scarlet macaw uses its hooked beak to eat fruit and nuts.

Hummingbirds drink flower nectar.

Down on the forest floor, a tapir looks for leaves and fruit to eat. It helps spread plant seeds to other areas of the forest when the seeds come out in its poo!

Who ate the butterfly?

A green basilisk lizard ate the butterfly. It spends most of its life sunbathing in trees near water.

The lizard eats lots of different foods including flowers, fruit, insects and mice.

To escape danger, the lizard will drop from its branch and run across the surface of the water on two feet.

?

?

?

Who ate the lizard?

An opossum ate the basilisk lizard. It came across the sleeping lizard and ate it up. Snakes and birds also like to eat lizards.

Opossums hunt for food at night and will eat almost anything, including dead animals! This one has found some bananas to eat.

An opossum mother carries her babies inside a pouch when they are tiny. When they are bigger, the babies cling to their mother's fur.

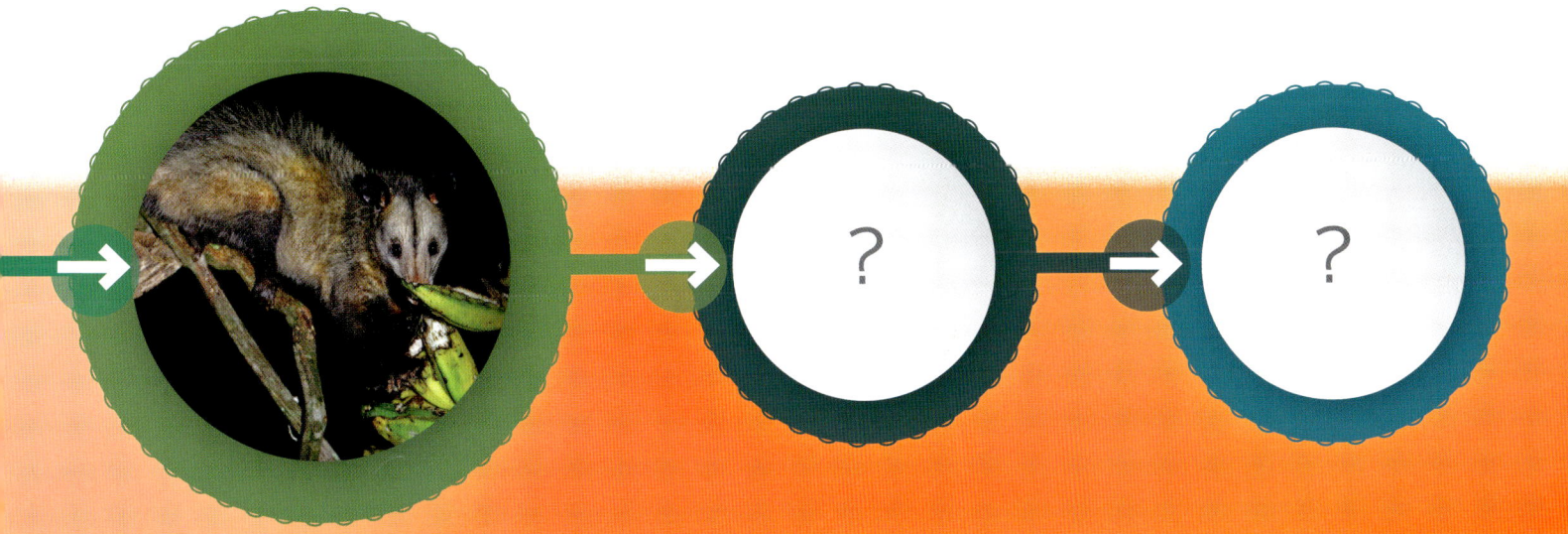

? ?

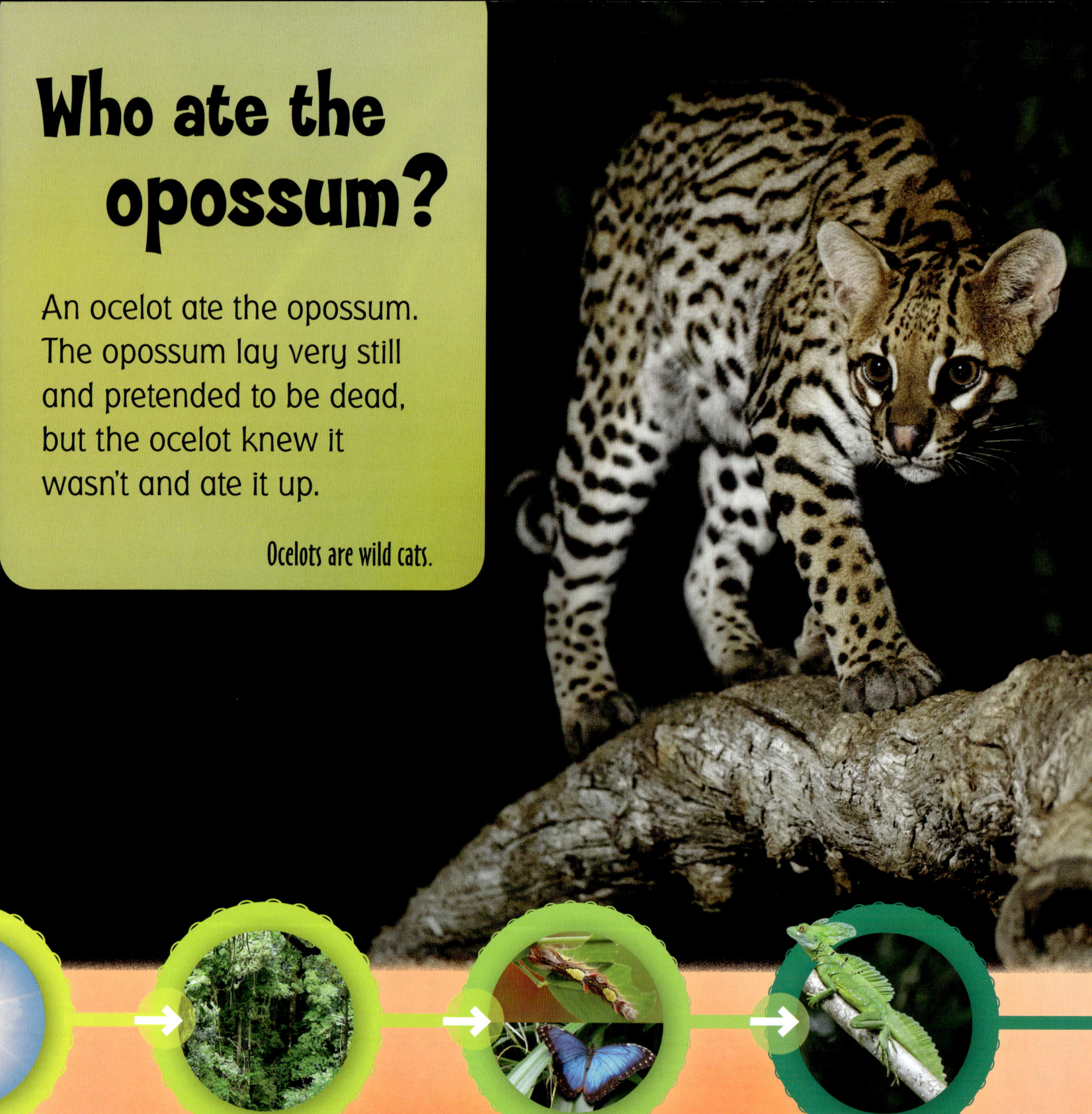

Who ate the opossum?

An ocelot ate the opossum. The opossum lay very still and pretended to be dead, but the ocelot knew it wasn't and ate it up.

Ocelots are wild cats.

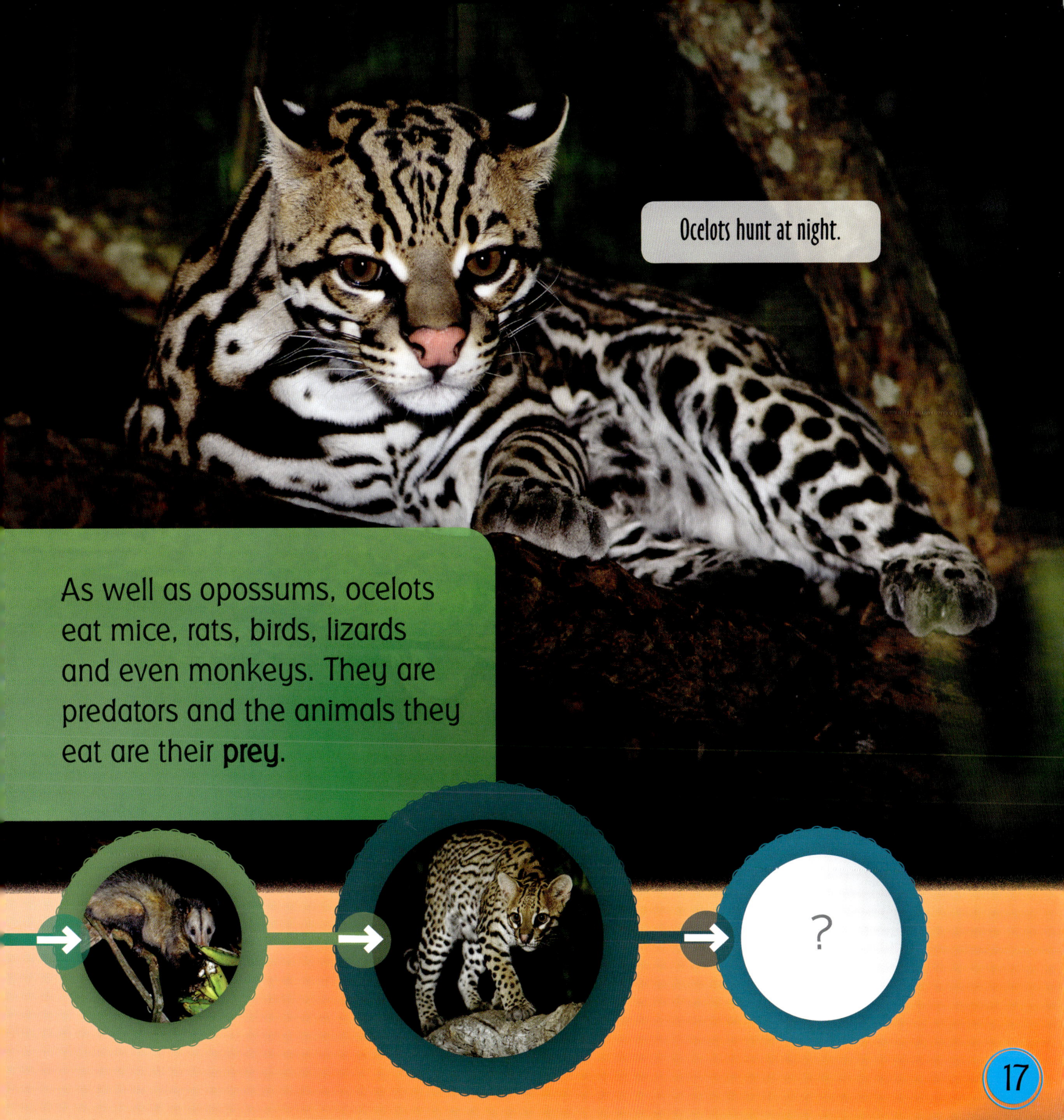

Ocelots hunt at night.

As well as opossums, ocelots eat mice, rats, birds, lizards and even monkeys. They are predators and the animals they eat are their **prey**.

?

Who ate the ocelot?

If a jaguar lives in the same part of the rainforest, it may kill and eat the ocelot.

Jaguar

In the past, people killed ocelots in great numbers for their beautiful fur coats. This happens less today as it is against the law in many countries.

In a rainforest, an ocelot usually lives for about 8 to 11 years.

Follow a rainforest food chain

There are many different food chains in rainforests. They all start with energy from the Sun that is made into food by the producers, the plants. The other animals are consumers. They eat animals, plants or a mix of both.

1

2

3

Can you remember the names of the links in the rainforest food chain shown in this book?

A rainforest food web

Who eats what in a rainforest can be shown as a **food web**. It is made up of lots of different food chains. Here is a simple food web including some of the animals in this book and a few others.

Basilisk lizard

Blue morpho butterfly (Caterpillar)

Seedlings

Opossum

Banana palm

Tapir

Howler monkey

Jaguar

Ocelot

Boa constrictor

If one link in a food chain is broken, it can affect the whole food web. Take tapirs, who are hunted by people for food. Tapirs spread plant seeds far and wide in their **dung**, so fewer tapirs means less **variety** of plants growing in the rainforest.

The biggest threat to all the wildlife in a rainforest is people. They cut down the trees and clear the land for farming. When rainforest is cut down, the animals and plants that lived there lose their home.

Useful words

bromeliad A plant that attaches itself to tree branches and gathers food and water from the air around it.

consumer An animal that eats plants, animals or a mix of these.

dung Another word for animal poo.

energy Food energy keeps a living thing alive and allows it to move, breathe or work in some other way.

food chain The plants and animals linked together by what eats what.

food web The food chains linked together by what eats what in a habitat.

fruit The part of a plant containing its seeds.

nectar A sweet liquid made inside plants' flowers to attract insects.

predator An animal that eats other animals.

prey An animal that is hunted and killed by another for food.

producer A living thing, such as a plant, that makes its own food using sunlight, air and water.

rainforest A thick forest where it rains a lot, often found in areas close to the equator.

seed The small part of a flowering plant that can grow into a new plant.

variety Several different sorts of the same thing.

Index

basilisk lizards 12–14, 21–22
birds 5, 10–11, 14, 17
butterflies 5, 8–9, 12, 20, 22

caterpillars 8, 20, 22
consumers 5, 8–23

food web 22–23
frogs 5

jaguars 18, 21, 23

monkeys 10, 17, 23

ocelots 16–19, 21, 23
opossums 14–17, 21–22

plants 4–11, 14, 20–23
producers 4–8, 20, 22

seeds 11, 23
snakes 14, 23

tapirs 11, 22–23